TAKE THE TILLER

Poems by
NIGEL PECKETT

APS Books
Yorkshire

APS Books,
The Stables, Field Lane
Aberford, West Yorkshire,
LS25 3AE

APS Books is a subsidiary of the APS Publications imprint

www.andrewsparke.com

I dedicate this book to my wife Sheila
together with Annique Seddon
and the following writer's groups:
Stafford Rising Brook Poetry Group
Stafford Rising Brook Writers' Group
Stafford Baswich Poetry Group

CONTENTS

Sadness

Seasons

The Dark Side

HUMOUR

BARBEQUE.

'It's a fine day.'
'Let's have a barbeque?'
'I'll get it organised'.'
I'll get some food'.
Mum's face falls
Remembering last summer's fiasco.
'Are you sure Dear? '
The dreaded word 'Dear'.
Dad goes to the shed.
Wheels forth the rusty, dusty barbeque
Complete with blackened griddle covered in last year's
rancid fat.
To the shops
Back with half a ton of cheap meat products
Specially designed to harden the arteries
The sun shines.
Mum's prayer for rain unanswered.
The barbeque is trundled to the centre of the lawn.
The worms burrow deeper.
The neighbours go indoors and shut the windows
The dog looks on hopefully.
The cremation fire is lit.
A heap of cheap charcoal.
Three firelighters, one pint of paraffin.
Just to make sure it burns.
To be sure of ignition the blow lamp is found.
Still sooty from last year.
The match is lit,
The blow lamp ignites with a roar.
Instant towering inferno.
No eyebrows for Dad.
An offering to the fire gods.
Half an hour later

Dad can get to within three feet of the fiery dragon.
'Get me the sausages please'.
The butcher's cheapest are brought forth.
Percy porker's innards are offered for sacrifice.
Thirty seconds they later are converted into charcoal.
Cheap buns, lots of cheap red sauce
Cannot hide the taste of paraffin.
As Dad looks away the dog is fed
Now for the steak
No tougher than a boot sole
The rain god takes pity and the heavens open.
The funeral pyre is extinguished.
Mum thanks the rain god.
In the kitchen bacon butties are cooked and eaten.
'We must do this again' says Dad
He doesn't know that the scrap metal man is already on
his way
Dad goes down the pub,
The barbeque goes on a one-way trip to the scrap yard.
Dad won't find out until next year.
Many stomachs praise the Lord.

Little Haywood, 25th March 2025

LARRY AND THE NIGHT OUT

On the street stood a drunk called Larry
On the street stood his friend Flash Harry
And nearby staggered their mate Gary
Waiting for the boozers opening
Listening for the door bolts pulling
And the people of the township
Welcomed them with jeers and laughing
Ate fish and chips, loudly shouted
Look! Those drunken, oafish, topers
They have drunk the strongest liquors,
Swigged the mighty fiery water
Dimmed the wits of their brain boxes
Which will lay them in the gutter
Making them to cough and splutter.
In the morning best forgotten
Woe to the thick head feeling rotten
Clothes all crumpled, tee-shirt sodden
Hair adorned with fag ash dusty
Wallet empty, eyelids crusty
All the trophies of the evening
Headache, stomach cramps and sickness
Comes heartfelt cry without thinking
'Never again will I go out drinking'

Little Haywood May 1st 2020

MAGAZINE RACKS

I creep into every living room
I slink into the library
I hide behind the armchair
I lurk behind the sofa
I crack shins under the coffee table
In the night I walk and stalk
Humans think they control us
How wrong they are
We breed in the dark and multiply
Our eggs are hidden as old receipts
Nestling in wastepaper baskets
Our larval stage is the coat hanger
Tangled in cupboards
Pupating we hide as old slippers

In our adult form
We sneak about collecting magazines
We seek out the junk mail
You will never see us move
We move by teleportation
Soon every house will be taken over
Alien visitors from far away
Or time travellers
Will find a world choked in paper
But neatly filed

We will conquer their spaceships

We are the future
The universe is ours

HAHAHAHAHA HAAA

Little Haywood, August 8th 2024

ODE TO THE QUAKER CHEF

If you have a Quaker chef,
It's better than a laxative.
For breakfast: baked beans, wholemeal toast and muesli too.
If you think that was bad then wait just wait for lunch.
It is the most dangerous of the bunch,
Just you wait and see:
Cabbage, cauliflower and the dreaded broccolee,
In addition to that lot, are onions, peas and shallot.
Just wait for tea and what do you see?
Green lentil stew and broccolee.
Just to go to bed!
(*If you dare*). The backfires blow the bedclothes in the air!
Morning comes, I draw a veil because in the toilet there is great travail.

Swarthmoor October 2014

THE SONG OF SUPERMARKET SHOPPER

In the store of Supermarket Stafford,
By the car park underwater.
Stood shopper looking discommoded.
Brown water his car had drown-ded.
At rain clouds of deepest blackness,
Wildly at the skies he shouted
Rude words that are best unspoken.
Yes, indeed his car was broken.
Full of water cushions floating,
Bonnet lifted engine flooded.
Comes A.A. man tow rope fitted
Wet car pulled out, shopper grateful.
Careless shoppers learn this lesson
When in Supermarket store of Stafford
Leave not your car unattended
Or it may become deep drownd-ded

Little Haywood 6th June 2016

THE FAR SIDE OF THE MOON

On the far side of the moon.
The stripey Piejams fly,
They do loop-the-loops and whizz through hoops.
At night they nest in loaves of bread
With toast and Marmite they are fed.
On the ground the Bruzzles love to ballet dance.
It's all very well but their skinny legs are eight feet tall
And with three left feet it's hard not to fall
For tea they eat curried jam with cheeses that sneezes
and then goes BANG.
On guard the fearsome Weasums stand by,
With dreadful, stinky breath and one big eye.
If you're threatened by an enemy, the Weasum turns
them to a deademy
If in the woods you may chance
Take a Weasum and a sprogling lance.
For in the jangled jungled wood, the awful, nasty
Sneakums lurk
Who shout rude words, steal your jam and then just
smirk.
If that wasn't bad enough;
Behind each tree hides a dreadful Huff
Are they brown or are they buff?
No, you see they just take snuff.
Better by far take my advice, it's really nice
Walk in the fields and see the pink sugar mice.
Stay upwind of the bloated Bong;
It's blotchy red with size fifteen feet that really, really
pong.
In the pens the Spriggits flumpy, jumpy ten feet high,
They chew up paper, string and eat stone pie
And when they're bored they play 'I spy'.
The grass is pink the sky is green.

The warbling Warjums just must be seen.
Don't forget the singing Sausage too, with its pickled
jerkin all in blue.
Now.
If on holiday you have to go.
Then zoom your parents to the moon
It's much more fun than Scragness-on-sea, with its soggy
chips and cold weak tea.

Swarthmoor October 2014

THE MEETING

Hands are shaken at the door,
In silence Friends file in and sit down.
The clock ticks out its measured pulse,
The silence gathers.
Stand up 'The sun is shining and the Spirit too'
Sit down
Stand up 'I saw a bird its breast was blue'
Sit down
Stand up 'Look out of the window, there's a Jay'
Sit down
Stand up 'My mother's ninety and is here today'
Sit down
Stand up 'Praise the Lord, hip hip hooray'
Sit down
Stand up
Keep moving
Sit down
Stand up 'I saw a daffodil, it must be spring'
Sit down
Stand up 'But only yesterday it was snowing'
Sit down
Stand up 'The peace of God passeth all understanding'
Sit down
Stand up 'It certainly does'
Sit down
STAY DOWN

Woodbrooke 3rd March 2016

MEMORIES

APPLE TREE

Low in the winter sky the orange sun
Old apple tree catches the light
Upheld by creased trunk
Shadows shape each branch
Frost melts drops shining
Each twig glistens
Unshed leaves holdfast
Moss greens in the light
Long shadows caress the grass

Woodbrooke 6/12/2014

A SCHOOL BOY

Tousled hair, big grin.
Legs racing,
Coat flying.
School bag chasing him.
Arms pumping,
Shoes pounding,
Gets there, just in time

Little Haywood 13th April 2000

DEPARTURE AND ARRIVAL

September nineteen sixty-four,
Bristol Temple Meads station
Brunel's Tudor Palace
One gangly eighteen-year old and parents
Luggage for university
Excited and nervous
Ticket office, green ticket, second class
The station smelling of sulphur, smoke and fish
Noise of iron wheeled trolleys loaded with goods
Noon
Soon the Devonian express will arrive
It arrives puffing like grampus
Hissing like a pressure cooker
The luggage loaded aboard the guards van
A hug and a kiss
The teenager gets aboard
Green flag and whistle.
A jerk as the train pulls off
He does not know it yet
He has left home forever
A milestone
Head out of windows waves
The station soon out of sight
Unfamiliar stations flash by
Time passes
Cheltenham, Gloucester, Birmingham, Derby, Sheffield
Finally Leeds the destination
Gets out, finds luggage,
Lost in the bustle of the platform
Ticket handed in
Finds a taxi.
Address on a bit of paper
Six o'clock arrives at digs

Tired nervous,
Meets landlady
Cup of tea,
A meal with the other students
Bed, breakfast
Today term starts
 A new life starts

Little Haywood 1ˢᵗ June 2025

JOURNEYS

Shortening days of autumn sun
Cool nights
Bright with Harvest Moon
Wire necklaced with martins
Chattering as they jostle for a place
Playing tag around the trees
Swooping to hawk drowsy flies
Then,
One day they are gone,
Called by a fiercer southern sun
My garden is quiet now
No gossiping in the eaves
No aerobatics in the sky
Earthbound am I
Waiting for Spring
And their return

Swarthmoor 6th September 2018

OLD BRUNO

Now I'm old I just don't care,
Tell me off and I'll just stare.
Leave the door and I'll sneak out
Wander round and make you shout.
I'll sleep in your comfy chair
And block up the Hoover with my hair.
Any food you leave around,
Will soon be in your faithful hound.
Where's the food for the cat?
Down the hatch, two seconds flat.
I may be old and may be slow,
I'll keep you out in frost and snow.
I'll dawdle with my dodgy hip
When out of sight I'll trot and skip.
Out on a walk I have a wooden ear
Call me back and I won't hear.
We love you still you scruffy dog,
Lie by the fire, sleep like a log.

Little Haywood February 16th 2003

SHETLAND SOAPSTONE BOWL

On the ground lies a bowl roughhewn,
Cast aside a thousand years ago.
A flaw discovered,
Thrown down.
Left on the white stone dust.
What were the maker's thoughts?
I pick up the bowl,
Cradle it,
Treasure it,
Picturing thoughtwise the carver;
A Viking freeman?
A slave chafing in thraldom?
The bowl speaks no words;
The mind flies back ten hundred years;
Seeing and unseeing the past.
The bowl is caged in a museum.
Does the onlooker feel the same,
A strong thread pulling the eyemind?
Time flows carrying memories floating on the stream for
the watcher
Who waits patiently, silently, wondering.

Little Haywood 21st July 2015

STRANGE HE WAS

Strange he was
To me, a small boy in the country
Smelling of tobacco and meals of long ago
Riding his big bicycle
Sitting upright, a knight on his charger

Strange he was
Ancient as the chalk downs
A spade tied to his bicycle like a couched lance
His large flat cap a helmet
His tweed clothes a suit of armour.

Strange he was
A noble come to dig our garden
Old he was
Survivor of an ancient war
A warrior burdened by memories

Strange he was
Timid almost silent
Living with his aged mother
In a small cottage with curtains drawn
Who grieved for her dead son killed long ago

Strange he was
Broken by the trenches and horror
Mourning for his brother
Killed in a slough filled hole
His name carved on a stone plinth

Strange he was
Pictured in my mind
A gentle man treating me as an equal

Talking in a quiet voice
A voice unused to speaking.

Strange he was
I remember him well
From my long ago
He lives on in my mind
A kindly man but strange

24th February 2023 Little Haywood

Note:
In the early 1950s I was a child living in the chalk downs in a small village near Newbury.

Mr Barker used to come and dig our garden and help paint the house. He rode a large sit up and beg bicycle with a spade and fork attached to his bike. He had a big brush moustache, a big flat cap and tweedy clothes complete with a turnip watch in his waistcoat. We had a large boxer dog who used to tease him by stealing the paint brush if he put it down or he would run off with his waist coat if he was digging. He seemed very odd to me when I was small. However, when I grew older my parents explained why he was like that. I suppose they were sorry for him and had him work in the garden for company because he had few friends in the village.

He survived the trenches in the Great War but he was shell shocked and his younger brother Aubrey(or was it Evelyn I can't remember) was killed in the war. He lived with his mother in a small cottage with the curtains half drawn. I have a vague memory that it was a typically Victorian, inside lots of ornaments and quite dark. He and his mother had never really got over the war. I suppose they were victims of the trenches.

TAKE THE TILLER

The holiday makers from the Brummagem factories
One week's holiday
Bed and breakfast seven and six a day
Fish and chips, beer, penny arcades.
Stop me and buy one
Kiss me quick
Pierrots on the pier
What did the butler see
High tide today but beach enough for all
Sandcastles, gritty sandwiches
Salvation Army parping and booming
Donkeys, cockles and whelks
The pleasure boats are queuing at the jetty
"Calm sea today missus"
"We're off to Flatholm"
"That'll be two bob a head"
Coins jingle
Boatman shouts "We're full"
The engine sputters and chugs
We're heading out across the Bristol Channel
Hands dangle in the salt water
The odd hat goes for a swim
Laughter, chatter and photos.
A small boy watches it all
Sitting by his dad
Fair haired and brown as a berry.
Jeans, tee shirt, Clarks sandals
A while later the keel scrunches on the beach.
The boatman helps the seafarers ashore
Laughing, giggling and larking
'Back in an hour mind'
Sounds like "Baack in an howerr Moind"
A west country twang

The boy helps dad refuel the tank.
An hour passes
"Get back aboard folks"
Homeward bound
Happy chatter
The jetty soon is reached
Too soon for the boy
The holiday folk leap ashore
Heading for the pub
On the boat dad says
"Take the tiller"
"Back to the mooring son"
"Point the bow at that rock over there"
"While I tidy up"
And there he is
Eyes squinting against the sun
The old Pier looms into view.
The Mona is buoyed and moored
Off home to tea on the open topped bus
The boy lives on forever.

11th July 2024 Little Haywood

TIME FOR PLAY

Endless blue skies of summer
Horizon stretching forever
Always sunny
Tee shirts, shorts held up by snake belts, Clarks sandals
Sun bleached hair and nut-brown faces
Dry chalky Berkshire Downs a playground
Wide leafy hedges hide our dens
Imaginations have no limits
Unseen we peep out as grown ups pass
As our minds go free in aeroplanes, ships, cars
Hazel cut by penknives makes bows and arrows
Whistles fashioned from elder
Or high oak tree branches hide us from view
Parents would chide if they saw us climb so high
Apple tree branches in gardens become Spitfires
Weaving patterns in the sky
Garden's soil is dry and dusty
Dinky toys build roads and race each other
Or dig holes as deep as the ocean
Lead soldiers build castles
Wide fields of wheat and barley baking in the sun
Smelling like toasting bread
We follow the reaper binder pulled by a blue Fordson
tractor
Building sheaves into stooks to dry in the sun
A wooden wain pulled by a tractor
The shire horses retired and almost forgotten
Shirt sleeved men pitchfork sheaves
Stacking them high on the wagon
Riding high we are caried to the rick yard
Sheaves are built into round thatched ricks
Meantime the forty-acre field is now our playground
Our legs scratched by sharp stubble

The hares run and jink for us as we play
Rooks and pigeons glean the fallen grain.
The thrashing machine arrives and sits waiting.
Boys watch as the drive belts are connected to a Fordson
The belts slap as the tractor starts.
All day men shout and feed the hungry machine
The tractor stops
A break
Drinking cold sweet tea from Corona bottles
Eating bread and cheese
Slap, slap all day long, the air dusty
Sacks fill with grain, chaff falls on to the ground
Straw is bailed
Ricks shrink until the machine stops
Rats and mice scamper from their nests
We put mice in pockets and take them home
Mum is not happy and the mice go free
Teatime of bread and jam
The whole world a playground
A summer that has no end
Eternal summer in my mind

Little Haywood October 1st 2025

PLACES

CUMBRIAN FELLS

Born long ago in fire and smoke
As high mountains I brushed the sky
Time, as it will, has my jagged bones worn down with
rain, frost and sun.
Twice (or is it thrice ten times?) the mantle of ice has
come and smoothed my rocky sides.
Now I lie beneath a counterpane of green.
Jaunty becks have carved brown niches in my hide.
Your grey towns and villages I hold in the palm of my
hands.
Sturdy farmhouses brave boisterous winds near my tops.
Close in-bye, small gardens grow roses red
Stone walls tattoo my skin making patterns seen from
            afar.
Your mottled shaggy sheep fair isle my arms.
Look close and under lumpen mounds are your dwellings
from long ago.

The seasons roll as mother earth swings round the sun as
moth chases the candle flame
Hot high
Warm wet torrents rain
Drifting continents
Covered in sea limestone
Lush forests coal

The high fells where you do not build or delve are
winter bare.
But come soft sun and springtime then my garland of
flowers grows.
High summer brings the bright heather with cotton grass
powder puffs.
Yet this season is short for August signals change.

Autumn bracken rusts and rustles in the wind.
Winter returns and my white coat returns.
For another year has passed.

I remember when forests were sea to sea
And man was content to roam and follow the seasons.

The seasons still roll as my mother swings round the sun
As a moth circles the light.

Swarthmoor Autumn 2014

NORWICH CATHEDRAL

A quiet chapel,
The walls holding nine hundred years of prayer.
Each stone brought many miles,
Shaped with skill.
Snugly fitting with its neighbour.
Slowly rising from strong foundations.
Reaching skyward.
Wooden scaffolding, simple tools, strong backs,
Tough, crafty hands.
Working month by month.
Season by season.
Year by year.
Thick pillars, graceful arches,
Carved bosses, grinning gargoyles,
Saintly figures and delicate windows.
Great timbers clothed with lead,
Defying the rain.
Glaziers bring bright glass,
Painters tell stories on the walls,
While the spire still rises.
Inside all is made well.
Fifty years.
The weathervane gleams atop the spire.
Bells peal.
Bishops, priests and monks sing.
Water is sprinkled, incense perfumes the air,
Bread is broken and wine poured.
The great work is hallowed.
In the nave the crowd marvel and rejoice.
Time passes.
And now I pray in silence,

Enfolded in peace,
While the sun warms my face,
Ignored by tourists chattering,
Forgetting what this place is.

Norwich Cathedral, Saint Catherine of Alexandria's Chapel
15th September 2015

ROOTS

Feet planted firmly on the grass
Rich soil holding me rooted.
I am owned by the land
By centuries of buried ancestors,
Sleeping in the churchyard nearby.
Protected by the nave and tower built by their hands.
Eyes looking at hills unchanged in five hundred lifetimes;
Hills clothed in copses and tracings of ancient lychetts.
The valleys full of small fields hedged by hawthorn,
Dressed in May time's white,
Or acres of open common land grazed short by kine and
sheep
Cross hatched with streams and footpaths.
Mellow honey-stone buildings sitting comfortably
together,
Corners rubbed smooth by time,
Resting in folds of the hills,
Sheltered by gnarled oaks.
Orchards of cider apples in bloom,
In the barns, last year's crop maturing in wooden vats.
In the distance the Severn winds greyly to the horizon.
This place remembers the past;
Stone hand axes unearthed in the autumn's digging,
Clay pipes, brass buckles and buttons.
Feet planted firmly on the grass,
Rich soil holding me rooted.

Little Haywood 5th March 2016

THE COTSWOLDS

Painswick, Cranham and Kitesnest Lane,
Valleys, hills laced with honey hued walls.
Minchinhampton, Nailsworth and Slad,
Commons, towns, snug cottages.
Hawkesbury, Inglestone and Lower Woods,
Celandine, wind flower and primrose.
Ozleworth, Selsley, Frocester Hill,
Wide open skies and narrow lanes.
Dursley, Stroud and Pucklechurch,
Furrowed fields and wooded copse.
Titherington, Dunkirk and Petty France,
Sheep, cattle and fallow deer.
Nympsfield and Hetty Pegler's Tump,
Steep hangers and shady streams.
Tetbury, Stow and Birdlip Hill,
Blackthorn, May and slender Ash.
Northleach, Bourton and the Slaughters,
Oak beamed pubs and quaint cream tea shops
Broadway, Kilcott and Wotton-under-Edge,
The Cotswolds are our privilege.

Woodbrooke 30th March 2015
Apologies to John Betjeman

THE FURNESS FELLS FROM CONISHEAD

Wind shepherds clouds.
White and grey as moorland sheep.
Gathering to their pen far across the sea.
Flat, wide waters of Morecambe Bay
Mirror the unruly flock's passing.
Sands wrinkle and twist in the setting sun.
Curlews pipe and prod the mud.
White gulls shine out.
Cormorant guards a rock.
Fells of Furness rim the view
Green and brown heather fading in the autumn's call.
Mist lightly veils the hills
Sun shouts from the clouds.
Mist turns to God's covenant with the Earth
Red, Yellow, Green, Blue.
Hills shine as glorious as stained glass in the sun
And dance in the joy of Light.

Swarthmoor October 2014
(See Psalm 114:4 and Genesis 9)

THE WEAVER HILLS

Here I sit in my thin place,
Where past and future have not yet been chosen.
Sun shines on sheep shorn grass.
Wind cats paws the uncut hay.
Buttercup, Tom Thumb, Lady's Smock and Day's Eye
Mingle with fescue, plantain and thistles.
Skylark carols the sky
Stone peeps through the turf
Showing the hills' strong bones
Who is sitting here now?
Who will sit here?
Who sat here?
Times all merging into one.
Each
Seeing the same sights,
Smelling the same smells
Hearing the same sounds
When is then?
When is now?
When?

The Weaver Hills, Staffordshire, 11th June 2015

THE WILD GOOSE

Last night I heard the Wild Goose call
Across the wooded land
As I watched the twilight fall
And the moon rose to light my way
Last night I heard the Wild Goose call
Did you hear it in your room?
Did you hear it in your dreams?
Will you hear the Wild Goose call
When you arise and greet the day?
When busyness of life seems all
Will you hear the Wild Goose call?
Last night I heard the Wild Goose call
It called to my heart and soul
I hear it still
Yes, I heard the Wild Goose call

12th May 2016 Swarthmoor

REFLECTIONS

AT DAWN NINE SWANS

Nine swans flying eastwards
Nine singing wings all in accord
Nine white companions
Nine necks outstretched
Nine wings outspread
Nine souls greeting the risen sun
Nine pilgrims
Nine, thrice sacred three
Nine, thrice three blessings

Swarthmoor 12th November 2015

COMPOSITAE CLASSIFIED

Compositae Bellis perennis
Now you are pinned and classified.
White, yellow, green
Confetti on my lawn.
Each flower a hundred florets,
Fused into one sunburst.
Compositae Bellis perennis
Names me not.
Call me 'daisy' and I may look.
Summer days and bees know me,
Whiteness, yellowness, sweetness.
Nighttime lullabies my sleepy eyes.
Compositae Bellis perennis,
Knows me not.
Made I was, long ago,
Mankind but a dream in the woods, a thought in
Creation.
He made and knew me,
Kissed me into life.
Compositae Bellis perennis
Not I

Swarthmoor October 2014

44

DESOLATION AND CONSOLATION

I stand in a desolate place
Soul stripped bare
Unshod
Bush burn for me
Speak out of the flames
Hallow the ground
Carve wise words on my soul
Lead me down from this place
Lead me out of the wilderness
To an oasis
Sanctuary
Quietness

A resting

From my cave I look out
The ground shakes
And wind howls
A gentle presence
A quiet voice whispering
Calms my soul
Feeds me
Leads me
Down to a safe haven
Stillness
Sanctuary
A resting
Before starting my journey
again

Little Haywood 11th May 2015
(Exodus Chapter 3 and 1 Kings Chapter 19)

EVENTIDE

Dimpsy
Warm breathed
Dark fells drifting into dreamtime
Edged by the sun's rose afterglow
Day's eye rests
Flittermouse hawks the dusk
Wakeful robin sings Vespers
Distant dog barks
Stars netted by oak-trees' lace
Sickle moon reaps eventide
Eternity in a moment
Eye-seen ear-caught
Heart embracing joy

Swarthmoor 10th May 2016

GREEN DESERT

Barley ripens in the sun,
Green desert stretching to the horizon.
Windwaves ripple the barley's beard.
No bright poppies to mar its face,
No skylarks or peewits sing here.
Ancient hedges torn up by the roaring, yellow dragon
To manufacture this flat, unlovely landscape.
Untended, unloved a hedge hangs on.
Here birds sing in defiance of the green,
Voles scurry in their private world;
In the small headland flowers bloom and creep down the
hedgerow.
Bluebells from the vanquished woods;
Foxgloves, primrose and wild strawberry from the
woodland ride.
Bindweed scrambles in the hedge, Dog Rose blooms.
Nesting birds flirt in the shelter of the straggling, unloved
hedge.
Eat we must but at what a cost.

Little Haywood 23rd July 2015

47

HOPE

Awaking to a new day,
Dreams fading,
Yesterday in the past,
Even the awaking passes,
Leaving dreamland behind,
Thoughts muster for the day ahead.
Remembering today's worries,
Heavy from yesterday
But they will pass,
All problems are resolved by time,
Washed clean,

All troubles pass
All troubles pass
All troubles pass

Yesterday's boulder
Crumbled away by time
Only a pebble today
Tomorrow only a speck
Let time wash away life's burdens.

Little Haywood 17 June 2024

LIVING WATER

Cup your hands,
Dip them in the Living Water.
This well never runs dry.
Be Prodigal,
Share it with all who are burdened.
Comfort those troubled or in loss,
Enfold them close,
The warmth of human touch brings more than words.
Tears flow, tears dry.
Hearts break and tear.
Every wound leaves a scar.
The balm of the Living Water,
Heals the wounded and bears the pain.
Oh you with this gift!
Fill your own wineskin too,
Quench your thirst.
Embrace all those in need.

Swarthmoor October 2014

SEEDLING OR FOREST

In the forest rooted in deep earth
Trees live, die and fall
In clearings seeds fall
On the fallow earth
Seedlings strive towards the light
Many wither untimely,
Others seek to choke all the forest
May our seedling reach the light
Grow in strength
And help sustain the forest of life

Little Haywood November 2010

STORM-RIDER

Far out at sea a storm
Hugs rage to itself
Lashing waves into striding hills
White horses racing on the crests
Stiff wings against the clouds
Breasting the gale
Foam-chaser on the unquiet sea
Wave-skimmer playing in the wild spray
Feeding on silver mailed arrows
Grey maalie at home on the unresting ocean
Passing from sight behind a curtain of rain

Swarthmoor 12th November 2015
(Maalie Shetland Dialect for a Fulmar)
(silver mailed arrows – herring)

THE FACE IN THE MIRROR

The face in the mirror looks back
Memories of more than seventy years look out
Peering out of a play pen
A summer's day in a tent
The smell of the canvas
The wide beach and sea
A little yacht on the boating lake
A donkey ride
The smell of both grandparents' houses
Cat wee, dog wee, Jeyes fluid, snuff and Woodbines'
smoke
A move to the Berkshire chalk downs
Wide skies, limitless horizon
A baby brother
Learning to ride a second-hand bike
Harvest time, stooking sheaves
A threshing machine with slapping belts
School, nature walks and lessons
A nativity play, Joseph with tea towel headgear
Decorating the pine scented tree
The coronation on a small screen
 A big dog and tabby cat
Model aeroplanes in plastic, tissue and balsa wood
The weekly bath water heated in the Burco boiler
Another move
Dorset hills and new friends,
Hills, streams and shingle beaches
Climbing huge beech trees
A grammar school and bullies
Yet another move, Kingswood Bristol
Father teaching in an Approved School
Mother on Fine Fare checkout
New friends, girlfriends, Saturday job

Studying for 'A' levels
Eighteen now and leaving home
Leeds University
Yorkshire moors, City centre, parties
Sharp smelling laboratories, lecture, exams
A wife, honeymoon and new job
Research in Birmingham,
Training to teach, teaching in a comprehensive
Holidays in the Shetlands
First house, first child, a son
Another job, another child a daughter
Another house last but one
Change job, change house.
The last house lived in for 40 years
The face looks out of the mirror
As do the traces and faces of seventy years

Little Haywood 18th August 2025

THE FOREST

Ten thousand leaf falls
Each season a heartbeat
Each year a breath
Countless manlives
Yet only twenty oaklives have passed
Since the ice left.
I covered the bare earth from shore to shore.
Northwards land darkling with pines,
Southwards broadleaved greened.
Sheltered by boughs deer foraged,
Beavers gnawed and wolves hunted.
Man roamed
Walking wide over the leaf strewings.
Knew me as Herne or sometimes Green Man
When I whispered in his dreams,
Telling secrets of the woods.
Man's heart turned.
Not content to take what was freely given.
My tall trees were felled and burnt for fields.
Now you push me back to the margins.
I wait as I have always waited,
Pass you will.
Just as the devouring ice.
I have eaten many proud cities
Nothing now but green humps and hollows
Where wild things rule.
I am patient.
I wait.

Little Haywood 8th August 2015

THE HOLY SPIRIT

The Holy Spirit is unchancy,
Not safe and warm.

Ebbing and flowing like the tide,
Who can hold the tide in their hands?
The wind blows where it will.
Who can hold the wind in their hands?
Wild as a wave breaking.
Who can hold the waves in their hands?
Flying as a wild goose high above.
Who can hold it back with their hands?
Falling as rain upon the ground.
Who can hold the rain in their hands?
Sun shining upon the earth
Who can hold the light in their hands?

The Holy Spirit is unchancy,
Not safe and warm.

Swarthmoor 14th November 2015
From: Under the Wave, Kanagawa by Katsushika Hokusai

THE JOURNEY

Time flows
And our passing is on this river.
The journey shaped by the flow.
Slow, majestic gliding over deep pools, under hanging
trees;
Jaunty, chattering to pebbles, singing to the sun;
Turbulent as rock strewn rapids;
Violent as a waterfall.

How will your craft travel this river?
Like a
Cockleshell o'erset by the first wave.
Bold boat breasting the foam
Floating feather, never sinking, carried into every
backwater, wash and eddy?
Twig cast up on the bank with other dry bleached sticks,
Washed slowly to the sea by each winter's flood.
The choice is not always yours to make.

My friend, whatever your vessel, you have a one-way
trip.
Enjoy the voyage,
Make friends of your companions
Greet the sun, wind and rain.
Savour the changing view.
As you travel from the mountain, across the plain, to the
estuary and the ocean.

Little Haywood 7th November 2000

TIME WAS AND WAS NOT

Time was and was not
No time passed for an eternity
Creation slept in dreamtime
Awaking in the nothingness
Light!
Thoughts passed and created
Matter formed and congealed
Liquid became liquid
Solid became solid
Life sprang forth greening the land and sea
Water, sun and moon nourished the green
Life, the great force, surged
Fish, birds and beasts sang and danced with joy in the
light
At last breathed man
Time was, and rested awhile

Little Haywood 19th April 2015
(Genesis, the creation)

TWINS

Inside each head
Dark and Light contend.
Laughing, crying, yearning,
Twisting, whirling, turning.
Dark seeking Light,
Light seeking Dark.
Dark shielding Light,
Light blessing Dark.
Eternal dancing twins,
Intertwined,
Separate,
Yet one.

Swarthmoor 13th October 2017.
First Poem since September 2016

WANTS OR NEEDS?

Man has many wants.
Possessions acquired are of little account;
They come and go like the fleeting rain.
Man has few needs.
Warmth, food, good company and friendship.
These are all that count.
All else is grist for the mill of time.

Whatever you recall
In the deep fastness of the night
While others sleep and you are wakeful
Places of happy times and comfort
They are make us what we are
Not our coveted belongings.

Little Haywood 27th January 2004

WORDS OR POEMS

(A poem for two voices: Hard and grating, *soft and gentle*)

My desk anvil hard
I sit in the sunlight
I forge words to my will
I catch my words from the breeze
My words are dark iron
My words live feather light
My words are tempered in the fire
I tend my words as tender seedlings
My words are riveted to the meter
Mine flow like water
My words are soon forgotten
Mine are eternal
Can you name the wordsmith
The gardener's words live on.

Little Haywood 4th April 2015

WORSHIP IS?

Worship is?
Sitting still in a silent room
Sitting with others
The room is quiet
Marooned in Silence
Or
Perfect timeless moments
A bee in a flower
A hover fly on my arm
Watching swifts playing
A beech tree in spring leaf
A frosty morning
A warm wood fire

Ministry is?

Words out of the silence
Or
Tending a garden
Cooking a meal
A hug
A kiss
Planting a tree

Swarthmoor 6th September 2018

YESTERDAY

'It's yesterday all over again'.
'Shit, shave and shower,
Breakfast toast and marmalade and tea.'
'Every day the same'.
How long had he had followed this routine.
Every day seemed gloomy.
But today the sun shone

A wind from the east.
Silver birches dancing in the wind.
'Bugger it, I'm going out.
I don't care what the weather does'.
'Hat, scarf, gloves and coat.
Scruffs, his dog, holding his lead.
Wagging his tail
Glad to see his master happy
'We'll take some snap
Cheese sandwich, flask, dog biscuits'

'Bugger it I feel alive again.'
The wind made Scruffs' ears flap
Albert scrunched his eyes in the cold wind.
'I wish Jenny was with us Scruffs,'
He walked through the new estate,
Across the rec
Through the kissing gate on to the moors.

'Scruffs let's go up Scar Crag.'
He let Scruffs off the lead
Off he ran,
Sticking his head down every rabbit hole.
Sneezing with excitement
'Daft Begger,' laughed Albert.
The wind swung northerly
 Bringing the smell of the moors

The rain started too.
'Sod it, I had hoped it would stay dry.'
Albert pulled up his collar and looked up to Scar Crag.
He had been there may times over the years.
Always with Jenny
'Muddy path up to the beck,'
He'd got into the habit of talking to himself
Swearing more now that he lived alone.

The path got steeper as he climbed
Up to the heap of millstone grit boulders.
Out of breath after the long climb
He reached the summit
Crowned by a concrete obelisk,
Stuck there by the Ordnance Survey.
As out of place as Arthur C Clarke's sentinel.
He sat down in the lee of a boulder
Got out his food and flask.
'Nothing like a bit of snap after a walk,
Scruffs got dog biscuits.
'Jenny would have enjoyed the walk,'.
'Best get going, got to get back for tea.'

He got up, felt tired, achy and short of breath.
'Out of condition, eh Scruffs?'
Out into the wind, now at his back,
He set off down the hill.
Halfway down he stumbled and fell.

Walkers found him.
They had heard Scruffs barking.
Albert's back against a boulder,
Smile on his face and guarded by Scruffs.

Little Haywood 1st July 2025

SADNESS

REMEMBER HIM AT HIS BEST

Together family and friends gathered in grief;
Parents outliving their dear child, friends with planned
joys cut short
All united, for a while, by untimely death.
Hugs, kisses, soft words and gentle tears
Six carry their fond burden.
Friends speak from their hearts, family recall the past.
Words of comfort, but he is gone never to return.
At last is body his borne on its last journey, short in
distance far in time.
We stand in the bitter wind and sleet
Chilled in body and heart, we say farewell
Down he is lowered into his last bed.
For remembrance, heather from his homeland
Is dropped by loving hands.
The company drift away in ones, twos and threes.
Warmth, we meet in warmth to eat, drink and
remember
Held, briefly in this room by life and loss.
We leave, the son, the lover, the friend;
In this place and time unexpected.
His mother said:
"Remember him, remember him at his best"

Little Haywood 6 April 2000
(Gavin's funeral)

REQUIEM FOR A CROW

I fledged late summer,
Wings untried, till coaxed by anxious parents,
I fumbled into the air.
Harvest gleaning of fallen corn,
Fat worms fed my growing strength.
With my playmates I cavorted in wide skies.
Soft winds and gentle sun bore me aloft.
Hills below, those mighty stones green garbed.
I gloried in my black armour, glistening in the early
autumn sun.
Comes October and a ruffian wind
Tossed me as a wizened oaken leaf.
It rode me down, my spurs yet untried,
It broke my youngling bones and cast me down.
I was felled from the unruly and unkind sky.
Here I lie, dazed in sodden grass.
No mate for me or chicks to hatch.
All too soon my summer's passed.

Swarthmoor October 2014

TWO REQUIEMS FOR UKRAINE

Two Summers

Under the summer endless sky

Rich grass, bright daisies, yellow buttercups
Placid cows graze
The shady woods play hide and seek
With children and shy animals
Golden fields
Waving catspaws chasing the warm breeze

Under the endless summer sky

Nearby, towns and villages
Drowse in the afternoon warmth
Grandparents sit in the shade
Recalling the past
Parents weed the garden
And smile at each other

Under the endless summer sky

Tomorrow comes
Time to gather the harvest
Yellow machines march in echelon
Garnering the golden grain

Summer reflected in a cracked mirror

Under the endless summer sky

Crushed wildflowers
Desolate fields

Shattered woods broken branches clawing the sky
Silent with menace
Fields of rich black earth
Barren and broken
The fields are churned
By great makers of death

Under the endless summer sky

Villages and towns
 Lie shattered as Jericho
Orchards barren
Gardens empty
Ovens cold
Hearts riven
Families flee eastward
All hope gone

Under the endless summer sky

Only the graveyards prosper
Testament to ambition and greed.

80 years pass

Two Winters

Under the grey and bleak winter sky

The Earth is sleeping
Cows snug in their byres
Trees dream of summer
The woods are still
Fields lie quiet under a blanket of snow
Awaiting the Spring sowing

Under the grey and bleak winter sky

Nearby, towns and villages
Turn their backs to the east wind
Families sit around the warm tiled stoves
And talk quietly
Gardens lie sleeping
Fruit trees slumber

Under the grey and bleak winter sky

Tomorrow comes
Time to prepare for Spring
The ploughs will turn the fertile earth
Ready for the Spring sowing

Winter reflected in cracked mirror

Under the grey and bleak winter sky

The fields lie fallow
Deserted and silent
Rent trees lie broken
Crushed with despair
The fields rutted by tanks
Sowing nothing but death

Under the grey and bleak winter sky

Villages and towns lie silent
Shattered walls
Eyeless windows
Shredded curtains crying in the wind
Cold the hearth
Chilled our hearts
Families flee westward

All hope gone

Under the grey and bleak winter sky

Only graveyards prosper
Testament to ambition and greed

Yet again the seasons turn
And tomorrow comes again

Little Haywood 31ˢᵗ March 2022

STRONGER NOW AM I

Stronger now am I.
The fiery past has forged and tempered the iron of my
soul.
Death violent has wrenched a stranger from this world,
A friend taken from the joy of life.
Grief and shock unexpected.
Pain, illness and the span of mortality emphasised.
Relationships have stretched
Some snapped and others endured.

Yet now I feel more secure
Within myself.
Stronger and more secure.
The passage of time
As a cataract in flood
Has worn away the jutting corners
Leaving the bedrock smoothed, polished and enduring.

Who can endanger the citadel of my mind?
I look out from a high window,
Few can come to me now
And disturb the peace within my realm.

Little Haywood 10th December 2000

THE HAVEN

In troubled times I fly to my secret place.
A paradise.
An Island within my heart,
Beaches swished with white lipped waves.
Tern and gull dance in the shimmer,
Otter sleeks his way ashore.
Green sea and northern islands.
We sit on purple heathersides and watch.
Many have sat here and caressed the view.
Friends I have brought mindwise to this place.
Now you have flown northwards to those other isles,
Where I cannot go.
Wait on your shore
And wait.

Little Haywood December 2007
(Written after Carol's funeral)

THE HAVEN REVISITED

Passing time
Leaves paradise unchanged.
Bitterness of separation
Caressed and embraced.
Bright sea
Beach softly seawashed,
Waders scurry in the shallows.
Heather's scent on the breeze.
Still I sit and wait and watch
Holding hands with the past.
Touching the loss,
Painful memory soothed.
Remembering, smiling,
Recalling, reflecting,
Your wisdom still mindfresh.

Little Haywood 6th December 2106

THE SEASONS

AUTUMN

Autumn comes in both red and gold
And shorter days sharply cold.
Tattered leaves drift and fly,
Capricious winds chase them by,
Untidy in careless drifts blown.
Swifts and swallows have long flown.
Robin sings a song so chill,
Bids summer to stay here still.
Apple trees ripe for picking,
Blackbird chides, tail a-flicking.
Hawthorn hedges bare of leaf,
Drowsy hedgehogs sleep beneath.
Farmers walk fields briskly now,
Stubble waiting for the plough.
Earth ready for winter sleep.
Shepherd guards his wayward sheep.
While folk wait for Christmas cheer
Hoping for a kindly Year.

Little Haywood 1ˢᵗ November 2016

RESTING

Black and white
No colours here
Earth Slumbers
Blanketed in white

Hedges crouched against the wind
Deep drifts choke the hollow way
Sheep hunker under walls

Frozen pond spiked with reeds
Fish deeply dreaming

Oak trees stand
Stark against the sky
Clasped by driven snow

Resting, waiting
For Spring's awakening
And the year's re-greening

Swarthmoor 6th September 2018

SAMARA'S SONG

The Autumn wind has come to play.
Come dance with me Ash tree says.
Rain washed grey my bark,
Limb lithe to dance with you.
Freshly dressed in russet hue.
All day they danced,
In tight embrace
They swayed back and forth.
Leaves and seeds away they blew.
Each seed carrying life anew.
One seed tired from the dance,
Sheltered in the grass all winter through.
Came Spring and Mother Earth
Stirred the life within.
A shapely sapling grew.
Year on year it grew in strength
Until a dozen man-lengths high
And ten more wide.
The Autumn wind has come to play ....

Swarthmoor 15th October 2017

SEASONS' WHEEL

Each season has its rewards
And its price
The pleasure of change
The price of change
Which is first the pleasure or the price?
Winter cold and clear
Trees gaunt and bare
Birds shrink from the wind
Seeking shelter from
Soil hard and dark
Bulbs warm a snug below
Cold fingers, cold face,
Shrammed and hunched shoulders
Warm fireside, hot meals
Low sun red and cool
Landscape crimson lit
Countryside crisp and clear
Yule comes and goes
Snowdrops show their white and green
Imbolc beckons the turning year
Earth welcomes longer days
Life pulses stronger now
Dormant plants awake
Celandine star the grass
Dark gives way to green
Through Ostara to Beltane fire
Life beats more strongly
Trees green and plants bloom
Birds sing day and night
Cuckoo, blackbird and lark welcome dawn
Nightly woodcock rode and nightjars churr
Life pulses through veins
Gloomy thoughts fly away

Long days and short nights
Litha when the sun is high
The Oak king returns
High summer and warm nights
Lughnasadh is here
Crops ripen apples and berries swell
August and Lammas pass
Harvest comes with Mabon
Barns are filled and cider pressed
Harvest home brings hope for winter
Nights lengthen day by day
Samhain celebrates with fires
The dead are honoured
The nights get longer still
Until midwinter's Yule
Welcomes the holly king
and the sun's returning

6th October 2025 Little Haywood

Yule: December 20-23
Imbolc: February 1-2
Ostara: March 19-21
Beltane: April 30 – May 1
Litha/Midsummer: June 20-22
Lughnasadh: August 1-2
Mabon: September 21-24
Samhain: October 31 – November

THE DARK SIDE

BLACK DOG

Black dog
Waiting in the shadows
Patient as death
Waiting for an opening
Dark eyes shining
Waiting for weakness
Growling in the gloom
Waiting for tiredness

Black dog
Sitting in the dark
Watching passing thoughts
Sitting in the darkness
Twisting thoughts,
Waiting in the shade
Patient as death
Black dog

Little Haywood 15th January 2020

BURNT OUT.
Requiem for the back-to-back

Coal black, ink black, pitch-black eyes
Staring
Toothless open mouthed
Silently screaming
Standing hunched against the sky
Waiting

Surrounded by derelict houses
Smashed windows
Curtains flapping in the wind
Jagged walls
Open roofs
Broken toothed cobbled streets
Smoking
Pyres of houses
Derelict gardens
Nettles, briars and stunted saplings
Melancholy Roses
Thistledown drifting in the breeze
No street life here
Only echoes of the past
No children playing
No gossiping
No clothes lines crossing the streets

The last house
Awaiting
Now
Just the heavy beat of diesel engines

Little Haywood 3rd April 2024

DARK SOLSTICE

Unset of black sun,
The dark stars are rising.

Dark dusk and dark moon rising
Dark sky with darker stars, holes in blackest night
Unshine through black velvet,
Un-eyes watch the constellations of black night

The falling of the light brings forth the dark
Dark unmind stalks the night.

Cold the dark and warm the light
Turns year on year
Turns season on season
Day on night.

Dawn of light will it come?

Which will prevail?

The Dark?
The Light?

The Dark?

The Light?

Little Haywood 19th October 2001

DEPRESSION

Brooding on the hillside
Crouched malevolent
Hunched against the noonlight
A drear copse
Full of gloom
Lidded yellow eyes in the shadows
Gnarled knuckled branches
Enravelling blackthorn claws
Rustling, sly, dead leaves
Hating two legs

Come red-eyed sunsink
Twilight
Dwimmerlight
Dark night
Sickly creeping moon shadows
Swollen with menace
Exuding desolation into the night.

Swarthmoor 10th May 2016

90

ESCAPE

Voice one: Harsh, interrogative   *Voice two:* Diffident, quiet

Voice one	Voice two
Name?	Jack/Jane Smith
Address?	23 Acacia Road
Town?	Blackstone
County?	Cleveland
Post Code?	CL 23 0YG
Date of Birth?	1st February 1957
Height?	5 feet 8 inches
Weight	11 stone 2 pounds
National Insurance number?	AB 01 02 03 Z
Tax Code?	200 K
National Health Number	345 876 9452
Passport Number?	897456387
Pause	*Pause*
Spoken more loudly	*Spoken more loudly*
Is this you?	Is this me?
	or?
Pause	*Pause*
	Is there more than that?
	Can I escape the numbers?
	Can you escape the numbers?

Little Haywood April 16th 2024

91

PAIN

Pain is my secret fear
Slinking in the dark hours
Ambushing my joy
Pain is my dreaded enemy
Some days far away
Thunder muttering in distant hills
Other days as hard and sharp as broken flint
There is no escape

Each has their own Gethsemane
Crying out for release
There is no escape
Better to look the enemy in the eye
Do not give in
Stare him down
Holdfast

Woodbrooke 13th May 2015

REFUGEE

Oppressed by war
Cruelty unimaginable
Towns turned to flames
Killing without pity
Families gather belongings
Fleeing from danger to danger
Fleeing from uncertainty to uncertainty
Fleeing from hunger to hunger
Fleeing from thirst to thirst
Cold nights and burning days
Camping in the filth
All our possessions spent
Crammed into the hold of a derelict
Cast adrift
Cast adrift
Adrift

Little Haywood 21st April 2015

REVENGE

A playground slight years ago
A childish insult that meant to cut
She saw the whitened face
And tight clenched fist
That showed the barb had stung
She felt his pain
And saw the hurt
Remorse flamed her cheeks
She reached out
Touched his arm
"I'm sorry", she said

He turned away
Shook her off
It burnt into his soul
Hugged to his breast
Replayed in his mind
Endless repetition
It was nurtured long
Revenge lit its fire
And kept him warm

But lonely
So lonely

Years passed as they will
He saw her walking with child and dog
He grabbed her coat
And vented all the garnered hate
Angry words, spiteful words
Revenge he had or so he thought
When he heard the child say
"Who was that horrid man"

"I have no idea
Just some sad, sad old man"

Revenge was a
Dish eaten cold, very cold

Little Haywood 15th July 2024

THE DARK BEHIND THE EYES

Walk into the darkness
Walk down in the darkness
Walk slowly
Unbar the triple locked door
In the dark lie untouched hoards
Look into the shadowed corners
Seek the dusty chests
This one holds feelings
Long locked away
Lift the lids
Joy, grief, anger, hate, love
All waiting for release
Lying in this casket are senses
Taste of lemon
Touch of soft skin
A red dawn
Cry of your first born
All held in the dark fastness
Retrace your steps
Leave all unlocked
Bring back your treasures
Into the light

Woodbrooke 12th December 2015

THE DOOR OR INTERESTING TIMES

Awash with apprehension
Knowledge of what is to come
A nexus of anxiety focused in a doorway
A walk along corridors
False bravery hides the fear
Telling stories, anecdotes, anything to fill the time
The door awaits and opens
Faces, trolley, injections, oblivion
Lights, muddled awareness,
Surface into pain
Ride back to the ward
Machines that bleep and measure
Oh for the oblivion of before
Visitors, anxious faces mirroring love
Talking, more bravado,
Night-time quietness,
You have survived again,
Reflections in the night.
If life is a journey
Then I am riding in an oxcart over cobbles

Stafford Hospital 14th January 2015

THE FOUR HORSEMEN
(A poem for two voices: Child & Adult)

Who are those horsemen riding, riding, riding by?
Look away my child heed them not.
But who are the horsemen riding, riding, riding by?
You are frightened and turn pale.
Who are the horsemen riding, riding, riding by?
You will know them soon enough when they go riding,
riding, riding by.

Will you name them as they go riding, riding, riding by?
Must I do this?
Yes you must.

Who rides the white horse riding, riding, riding by?
That is Pestilence the cruel.
Who rides the red horse riding, riding, riding by?
That is War drenched in hot blood.
Who rides the black horse riding, riding, riding by?
That is Famine he devours all.
Who rides the pale horse riding, riding, riding by?
That is Death he will greet us all.

Who brought them here riding, riding, riding by?
Mankind himself brought them here my child.

Why is Pestilence riding, riding, riding by?
Damp and cold and filth.
Why is War riding, riding, riding by?
Power and lust and covetousness.
Why is Famine riding, riding, riding by?
Poverty and greed and selfishness.
Why is Death their companion, riding, riding, riding by?
Pestilence, War and Famine brought him here.

Must they always be here riding, riding, riding by?
When will they go riding, riding, riding, far away?

When mankind is wiser.
They will go riding, riding, far away
When mankind is kinder.
They will go riding, riding, far away
When mankind is giving.
They will go riding, riding, far away
When mankind is loving.
They will go riding, riding, far away

Little Haywood 18th November 2014

TODAY

Today colours are washed away, muted
The thick grey clouds have stolen colour
Drizzle falls and the land is drear and grey
The hills are hidden by the mist
Where is the warm sun
To brighten my day.
Water drips from flowers and leaves
Birds sit forlorn
Like bedewed thistledown
Even the bees are hived.
The land is silent
Sound is squashed, deadened
As if my head were under blankets
Hiding from the world in my own drabness
Cold seeps through my pores
And holds me fast
Where is the bright sun
Where are the colours
Where is the warmth
Where is life

Little Haywood February 2025

WILDERLAND

Skyrimmed saw-toothed hoary mountains
With icy slopes and bone chilling cold,
Where wyrms brood golden hoards
Bleak moors, peat hags and wind hunched rowan
woods.
Cliffs and strands wave clashed.
Grim shrouded oak wildwoods
Cut by deep, dark valleys
Riven by cataracts
Untame, wild, fierce
Unman friendly, man losing.
Ruled by the old gods
Wyrd guards it,
Wyrdings walk it.
A place of wild things,
Be aware, uneasy as a hare.
Man brings his own peril.
Come to Wilderland, it is near and far.
Lid your eyes and step in.
Wilderland is easy to find but hard to leave.
You leave not unchanged.

Tatton Park 14 June 2015

WINTER STORM

Dawn wakes with the red eye of wrath
Shadowed clouds crouch in the far hills
The vanguard of winter charges
With a bitter press of wind driven snow
Lone trees hunch their backs to the wind
Yellow eyed wolves cast baleful glances
Sheltered deep amongst the trees
Storm crows dance in the rising gale
Weatherwise shepherds gather their flocks
To shelter behind drystone walls
Fields are abandoned to winter's rage
Woods nestle in the hills
Low farms lie in the arms of the land
The ravening storm sets on
Roaring its fury at the warmth of life
Dry leaves flee the storm's charge
Quivering in dark corners
Too late for the tardy stockman
Whose cattle cower before the stinging ice shards
Snow strikes the waiting buildings
Bone biting cold gnaws at the sturdy farms
Peering with lidded eyes through shuttered windows

Little Haywood 5th April 2024

TIME AND TIDE

A BEACH

A beach.

Soft sand and pebbles
Waves washing the tide line
Seaweed swaying back and forth
Swash of waves on sand
Hiss of foam
Pebbles scurrying up and back
Clattering, chattering to the waves
Sounds as old as the Earth

Rock born long ago in Earth's furnace
Volcanoes' castles ringed with flaming ramparts
Yet even the hottest fire cools
Lava hardening into grainy granite

Gnawed by sun, rain, frost and ice
Seafists thrown by wind's fury
Stormy seafingers clawing rock lumps from the cliffs
Boulder pounding boulder
Pebbles grinding pebble
Soft sea or winter's gale
Yearly wearing pebbles to fine sand

Slowly drifting continents
Carry sand back to the fire
To start the journey over again.

A beach…

Rosemarkie 19 August 2015

EARTH CYCLE

Earth great turning
Season follows season
Never returning
Spring fresh greening
Summer fast ripening
Autumn leaf falling
Winter frost freezing
Never returning
Sun arising
Night asleeping

Tide ebbing, flowing
Beach daily revealing
Saltings refreshing
Observer watching

Never returning.

Swarthmoor April 8th 2019

EBB AND FLOOD

The eye follows the ebbing tide
Grey water giving way to sandy banks
Oystercatcher scurry back and forth
Chiding the tide away
Curlew their haunting call
Black cormorants stand statue still
Still the eye follows the retreating tide
Heartfelt loss of moving water
The water recedes to the setting sun
Taking driftwood on its endless journey
The watcher waits
For tomorrow the tide returns
To start the cycle yet again

Swarthmoor April 8th 2019

HEARTBEAT

Two slow beats a day
Rhythmic tide
Sly, grey fingers creeping
Sandbanks ever, never changing
Washed clean of footfall
Patient birds
Watch the waters edge
Ready for the flood
To lay siege to their refuge
Wave-riders in the van.
Yet soon
Ebb withdraws its outliers
Back to the grey whales' home
Leaving sea-washed sand
To whaup and white seamew
Regular, irregular
No two beats the same

Swarthmoor 6th September 2018
(Whaup – curlew Seamew – gull)

SPRING TIDE

Tar black, char black land
Lit by white bright moon
Land, sea and shore slumber

On the mud boats sleep atilt
Strand, sand, saltings lie quiet
Deep dark rock pools dream

Sea lies waiting offshore
Rippled, cats pawed
by gentle wind

Sun and moon conspire
With slack sea, salt sea
To inundate the land

Ebb has ceased
Slack water waits

Then
Slowly, slowly, flood awakes
Stars shine on soft silky water
Slyly, slinking, slithering landwards.

Flood strengthens
Muttering, whispering in sinuous sikes
Spreading wider
Seaweed, sand, stones submerge

Creeping, sneaking, drowning
Up to the high-water mark
Lapping seawall and pier

Then
High tide, sly tide.
Slip, slip, slides away

Jet black, wet black land
Lit by bright white full moon
Land, sea and shore slumber

Little Haywood 24th February 2024
Dialect: sike - rill, ditch

SUN CYCLE

The sun journeys the sky
Daily dawnings and sunsinks shift
Long days
Short nights
Short days
Long nights
Telling the passing of time

Bright sun daytimes
Cold moon lights the night
Rocks grow and wear away
Tides move
Sap-blood ebbing and flowing
Slow living trees leaf and unleaf
Measuring lives in leaf falls
Quick living warm-bloods.

Diurnal rhythm measured in heartbeats

Swarthmoor April 8th 2019

TIDE CYCLE

Eye follows the ebbing tide
Grey water giving way to sandy banks
Piping oystercatchers bustle back and forth
Chasing the sea away

Curlews haunting call
Black cormorants statue still
Still the eye follows the retreating tide
Heartfelt loss of moving water
The water recedes to the setting sun
Taking driftwood on its endless journey
The watcher waits.

For tomorrow the tide returns
To start the cycle yet again

Swarthmoor April 8th 2019

TIDE

Tide turns from slack to flood
Grey fingers slide over sand and mud
On the sandbars sombre cormorants shuffle back from
the rising water
Full flood and the tide gathers strength
Buoys lean against the flow
Water guggling in their wake
Boats strain at their moorings
Turning seawards anxious to be away
Like leashed hounds on a scent
Sandbanks drown
Slowly, slowly the tide creeps to high water

Flood turns to slack and then to ebb
Boats swing and face landwards
Buoys lean against the flow
Water guggling in their wake
Sandbanks surface
Cormorants usher back the tide
Piping oystercatchers stab the sand
Turnstones flip seaweed and clatter pebbles
The grey fingers slink back to the sea
Gathered back to its clenched hand
The watcher sees it and waits

Tide turns from slack to flood.....

Aberdovey 19th October 2015

WAVES

Far, far from land

Storm rages at the sail road
Wind strikes with galed fist
Waves, storm spawned
Hissing with fury
Racing the wind landwards
Beating the strand with hate
Blow after blow

But time cools their frenzy
Leaving pebbled washed beach
Glistening with wetness
Sun burnished sea washed.

Far, far from land ......

Swarthmoor 9th April 2019

114